The Hole Truth!
Underground
Animal Life

Burrowing Owl's Hideaway

by Dee Phillips

Consultants:

Mike Mackintosh
President of the Burrowing Owl Conservation Society of British Columbia

Kimberly Brenneman, PhD
National Institute for Early Education Research, Rutgers University, New Brunswick, New Jersey

BEARPORT
PUBLISHING

New York, New York

Credits

Cover, © Christian Vinces/Shutterstock and © Konstantnin/Shutterstock; 2–3, © Tania Thomson/Shutterstock and © OlegSam/Shutterstock; 4, © Filatov Alexey/Shutterstock; 5, © Tier und Naturfotografie/SuperStock; 7, © Richard Fitzer/Shutterstock; 8T, © Max Allen/Shutterstock; 8B, © Jaana Piira/Shutterstock; 9, © Jason Patrick Ross/Shutterstock and © Richard Fitzer/Shutterstock; 10T, © Jason Mintzer/Shutterstock; 10B, © Tom Vezo/Minden Pictures/FLPA; 11, © Roberta Olenick/All Canada Photos/Superstock; 12, © Roberta Olenick/All Canada Photos/Superstock; 13, © Malcolm Schuyl/FLPA; 14, © Mike Mackintosh/Owl Conservation Society of British Columbia; 15, © Zuma Press Inc./Alamy; 16, © James Urbach/Superstock; 17, © Mike Mackintosh/Owl Conservation Society of British Columbia; 18, © Donald M. Jones/Minden Pictures/FLPA; 19, © Phyllis Greenberg/Animals Animals; 20–21, © James Urbach/Superstock; 22, © Henk Bentlage/Shutterstock, © Margaret M. Stewart/Shutterstock, © Ralph Clevenger/Corbis, and © Frank L. Junior/Shutterstock; 23TL, © David Nagy/Shutterstock; 23TC, © Micha Klootwijk/Shutterstock; 23TR, © Rosalie Kreulen/Shutterstock; 23BL, © Jason Patrick Ross/Shutterstock; 23BC, © viceralimage/Shutterstock; 23BR, © Birdiegal/Shutterstock.

Publisher: Kenn Goin
Editorial Director: Adam Siegel
Editor: Jessica Rudolph
Creative Director: Spencer Brinker
Design: Emma Randall
Photo Researcher: Ruby Tuesday Books Ltd

Library of Congress Cataloging-in-Publication Data
Phillips, Dee, 1967- author.
  Burrowing owl's hideaway / by Dee Phillips.
     pages cm.—(The hole truth! : underground animal life)
  ISBN 978-1-62724-307-0 (library binding : alk. paper)—ISBN 1-62724-307-0 (library binding : alk. paper)
  1. Burrowing owl—Juvenile literature. 2. Burrowing owl—Habitations—Juvenile literature. I. Title. II. Series: Phillips, Dee, 1967- Hole truth!
  QL696.S83P445 2015
  598.9'7—dc23
                          2014021167

For more information, write to Bearport Publishing Company, Inc., 45 West 21st Street, Suite 3B, New York, New York 10010. Printed in the United States of America.

10 9 8 7 6 5 4 3 2 1

Contents

Meet a Burrowing Owl 4

All About Burrowing Owls......................6

An Underground Hideaway....................8

An Owl Goes Hunting 10

An Underground Nest 12

A Burrow for Eggs 14

A Burrow for Chicks 16

Hungry Owl Chicks................................18

The Chicks Grow Up 20

Science Lab...22

Science Words 23

Index 24

Read More 24

Learn More Online 24

About the Author 24

Meet a Burrowing Owl

It's early evening on a **grassland**.

A small bird with big yellow eyes appears from a hole in the ground.

It's a male burrowing owl leaving his underground home.

His family stays safe in the **burrow**.

The male owl will fly across the grassland to catch food for them.

grassland

burrowing owl

burrow

Burrowing owls sleep, stay safe from enemies, and raise their chicks in burrows.

All About Burrowing Owls

There are about 200 different types of owls.

Most owls build their nests and rest in trees.

Burrowing owls, however, live in dry, open places with lots of grass.

There are few trees in these places.

So burrowing owls rest and make their nests underground.

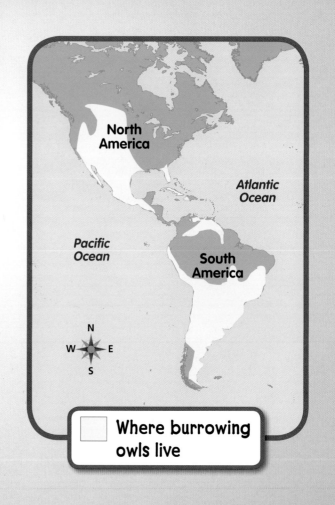

North America

Atlantic Ocean

Pacific Ocean

South America

N
W • E
S

Where burrowing owls live

An adult burrowing owl is about 12 inches (30.5 cm) tall.

How would you describe a burrowing owl to someone who has never seen one?

An Underground Hideaway

For part of the year, burrowing owls live alone.

When an owl needs to sleep, it searches for an underground hideaway.

It might find a burrow dug by a badger or some prairie dogs.

If the burrow is no longer being used by other animals, the owl moves in.

After resting, the owl leaves its burrow to hunt.

a badger digging a burrow

a prairie dog at its burrow entrance

An Owl Goes Hunting

Burrowing owls hunt animals such as mice, rabbits, lizards, small birds, and **insects**.

Sometimes an owl will sit on a large rock and carefully watch the grassland.

When it spots a small animal in the distance, such as a lizard, the owl takes flight.

It swoops down and grabs the lizard with its **talons**.

an owl watching the grassland

This owl has caught a lizard.

Burrowing owls can also hunt insects, such as crickets, by running after them. Other times, owls grab flying insects in midair using their talons.

cricket

talons

11

An Underground Nest

In spring, male and female burrowing owls come together to **mate**.

The two owls find an empty burrow where they will raise their young.

Using their beaks, the owls carry dry grass into the burrow.

They make a cozy bed with the grass.

This will be a nest for their eggs.

dung

Burrowing owls put animal poop, or dung, inside their burrow and around the entrance. Beetles that like to eat dung come to the burrow, which makes it easy for the owls to catch and eat them.

a pair of owls at their burrow entrance

A Burrow for Eggs

About 12 days after mating, a female owl lays an egg in her nest.

She sits on the egg to keep it warm.

Two days later, she lays a second egg.

She continues to lay an egg every one to two days until there are about nine eggs.

During this time, the female owl stays in the burrow to keep the eggs warm.

burrowing owl eggs

A female owl doesn't leave her eggs, even when she's hungry. She gets some food by eating beetles that come to feed on the dung in the burrow. In what other way do you think she gets food?

Animals such as badgers, skunks, and snakes eat owls and owl eggs. If a **predator** comes near the burrow, the male owl tries to frighten the attacker away. He spreads his wings and makes hissing and screaming noises.

a male owl scaring a badger away from a burrow

A Burrow for Chicks

While the female owl keeps her eggs warm, the male owl guards the burrow.

He also goes hunting and brings back food for the female.

About 28 days after the eggs are laid, the first owl chick hatches.

Over the next few days, the other chicks hatch.

male owl with food

female owl

newly hatched
owl chick

Baby owls have
just a few white, fluffy
feathers. The mother owl stays
underground with the chicks
to keep them warm with
her body.

one-day-old
owl chick

Hungry Owl Chicks

In the burrow, the mother owl eats the food brought by the father owl.

Then she spits up some of the food as a mushy meal for the chicks to eat.

When the chicks are about four weeks old, they have lots of warm feathers.

Now the mother owl can leave them to go hunting.

The chicks wait at the burrow entrance for their parents to bring back food.

four-week-old burrowing owl chicks

How have the owl chicks changed from when they first hatched? How are they similar to and different from their parents?

a mother owl feeding
a worm to a chick

Parent owls
hunt day and night to
find food for their chicks.
They rest only for short
periods of time.

The Chicks Grow Up

At four weeks old, owl chicks spend time exploring outside.

They also start practicing to fly.

Once the owls are seven weeks old, they can chase and catch insects on the ground.

During summer, the young owls' adult feathers grow.

By fall, the owls are ready to leave their parents and begin their grown-up lives.

an owl chick practicing flying

Science Lab

A Burrow Home

Like burrowing owls, the animals pictured below make their homes underground.

Choose one of the animals below and then use books and the Internet to research how it lives.

Next, make a chart to compare and contrast a burrowing owl with the animal you've chosen.

A burrowing owl and a badger

Things that are the same	Things that are different
Burrowing owls and badgers both live on grasslands.	A burrowing owl is a bird, while a badger is a mammal.
Burrowing owls and badgers both raise their babies in burrows.	An owl mom lays eggs, while a badger mom gives birth to live babies.

prairie dog

chipmunk

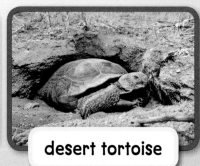

desert tortoise

badger

Science Words

burrow (BUR-oh)
a hole or tunnel dug by
an animal to live in

grassland (GRASS-land)
a dry place with a lot of
grass; only a few trees
and bushes grow there

insects (IN-sekts) small
animals that have six legs, an
exoskeleton, two antennae,
and three main body parts

mate (MAYT) to come
together in order to
have young

predator (PRED-uh-tur)
an animal that hunts and
eats other animals

talons (TAL-uhnz)
the sharp claws of
a hunting bird

Index

burrows 4–5, 6, 8–9, 12–13, 14–15, 16, 18, 22

chicks 5, 16–17, 18–19, 20–21, 22

dung 12, 14

eggs 14–15, 16–17, 22

feathers 17, 18, 20

female owls 12–13, 14, 16–17, 18–19, 21

flying 4, 10–11, 15, 20

food 4, 10–11, 12, 14, 16, 18–19, 20

grasslands 4, 10

hunting 4, 8–9, 10–11, 16, 18–19, 20

male owls 4, 12–13, 15, 16, 18

mating 12, 14

predators 5, 15

talons 10–11

Read More

Gilbert, Betty. *Buffy the Burrowing Owl.* Tallahassee, FL: Father & Son Publishing (2009).

Parker, Steve. *Owls (I Love Animals).* New York: Windmill Books (2011).

Phillips, Dee. *Spotted Owl (Treed: Animal Life in the Trees).* New York: Bearport (2014).

Learn More Online

To learn more about burrowing owls, visit **www.bearportpublishing.com/TheHoleTruth!**

About the Author

Dee Phillips lives near the ocean on the southwest coast of England. She develops and writes nonfiction and fiction books for children of all ages.